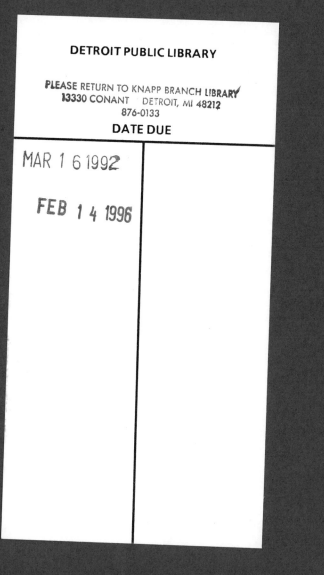

a poison tree and other poems

a poison tree

and other poems   illustrated by Mercer Mayer

Charles Scribner's Sons • New York

To Anne Diven

Copyright © 1977 Mercer Mayer

Library of Congress Cataloging in Publication Data
Main entry under title:
A poison tree and other poems.
SUMMARY: Twenty poems about such emotions as fear,
hate, love, delight, and guilt by a variety of English
and American poets.
1. Children's poetry, English. [1. English poetry—
Collections. 2. American poetry—Collections]
I. Mayer, Mercer, 1943-
PN6110.C4P57   808.81'9'3   76-57732
ISBN 0-684-14904-4

1 3 5 7 9 11 13 15 17 19 XD/C 20 18 16 14 12 10 8 6 4 2

Printing by Pearl Pressman Liberty
Binding by A. Horowitz & Son

Printed in the United States of America

Acknowledgments

"Albert" by Dannie Abse: Reprinted by permission of Anthony Sheil Associates Limited.

"The Black Pebble" by James Reeves: From *The Blackbird in the Lilac* by James Reeves, copyright © 1952 by James Reeves, published in 1952 by the Oxford University Press. Used by permission of the author.

"Boy at the Window" by Richard Wilbur. Copyright, 1952, by The New Yorker Magazine, Inc. Reprinted from *Things of This World* by Richard Wilbur by permission of Harcourt Brace Jovanovich, Inc.

"The Boy Fishing" by E. J. Scovell: From *The River Steamer.* Reprinted by permission of Barrie and Jenkins, Ltd.

"Forgive My Guilt" by Robert P. Tristram Coffin. Copyright © 1949, by The Atlantic Monthly Company, Boston, Mass. Reprinted by permission of the author.

"The House Plants" by Elizabeth Coatsworth: From *The Sparrow Bush* by Elizabeth Coatsworth. Copyright © 1966 by Grosset & Dunlap, Inc.; © copyright Elizabeth Coatsworth. Used by permission of Grossett & Dunlap, Inc. and by kind permission of Mark Paterson on behalf of Elizabeth Coatsworth.

"I Feel Me Near to Some High Thing" by William Ellery Leonard. Reprinted by permission of Gordian Press Inc.

"In the Night" by James Stephens: From *Singing Wind: Selected Poems* and *Collected Poems.* Copyright 1915 by Macmillan Publishing Co., Inc.; renewed 1943 by James Stephens. Reprinted by permission of Mrs. Iris Wise, Macmillan London and Basing-stoke, Macmillan Publishing Co., Inc.

"Loneliness" by Brooks Jenkins. Copyright 1935 by Scholastic Magazines, Inc. Reprinted by permission of the publisher.

"My Papa's Waltz" by Theodore Roethke: From *Collected Poems of Theodore Roethke.* Copyright 1942 by Hearst Magazines, Inc. Reprinted by permission of Doubleday & Company, Inc. and Faber and Faber Limited.

"Poem" by Langston Hughes: From *The Dream Keeper and other poems* by Langston Hughes. Copyright 1932 and renewed 1960 by Langston Hughes. Reprinted by permission of Random House, Inc.

"A Poem for Carol (May She Always Wear Red Ribbons)" by Nikki Giovanni: From *My House* by Nikki Giovanni. Copyright © 1972 by Nikki Giovanni. Reprinted by permission of William Morrow & Co., Inc.

Contents

A Poison Tree

I was angry with my friend:
I told my wrath, my wrath did end.
I was angry with my foe:
I told it not, my wrath did grow.

And I watered it in fears,
Night and morning with my tears;
And I sunned it with smiles,
And with soft deceitful wiles.

And it grew both day and night,
Till it bore an apple bright;
And my foe beheld it shine,
And he knew that it was mine,

And into my garden stole,
When the night had veiled the pole:
In the morning glad I see
My foe outstretched beneath the tree.

William Blake

A Small Discovery

Father,
Where do giants go to cry?

To the hills
Behind the thunder?
Or to the waterfall?
I wonder.

(Giants cry.
I know they do.
Do they wait
Till nighttime too?)

James A. Emanuel

A Poem for Carol
(May She Always Wear Red Ribbons)

when i was very little
though it's still true today
there were no sidewalks in lincoln heights
and the home we had on jackson street
was right next to a bus stop and a sewer
which didn't really ever become offensive
but one day from the sewer a little kitten
with one eye gone
came crawling out
though she never really came into our yard but just
sort of hung by to watch the folk
my sister who was always softhearted but able
to act effectively started taking milk
out to her while our father would only say
don't bring *him* home and everyday
after school i would rush home to see if she was still
there and if gary had fed her but i could never
bring myself to go near her
she was so loving
and so hurt and so singularly beautiful and i knew
i had nothing to give that would
replace her one gone eye

and if i had named her which i didn't i'm sure
i would have called her carol

20 dec. '71

Nikki Giovanni

In the Night

There always is a noise when it is dark!
It is the noise of silence, and the noise
of blindness!

The noise of silence, and the noise of blindness
Do frighten me!
They hold me stark and rigid as a tree!

These frighten me!
These hold me stark and rigid as a tree!
Because at last their tumult is more loud
Than thunder!

Because at last
Their tumult is more loud than thunder.
They terrify my soul! They tear
My heart asunder!

James Stephens

I Feel Me Near to Some High Thing

I feel me near to some High Thing
That earth awaits from me,
But cannot find in all my journeying
What it may be.

I get no hint from hall or street,
From forest, hill, or plain,
Save now a sudden quickening of my feet,
Now some wild pain.

I only feel it should be done,
As Something great and true,
And that my hands could build it in the sun,
If I but knew.

William Ellery Leonard

The House Plants

The house plants always have
                    a look
Of prisoners staring through
                    the bars,
They miss the air and
                    grass and stars.

And so I always talk
                    with them,
And touch them with
                    my softest hand,
To show them that I understand.

Elizabeth Coatsworth

Simple-song

When we are going toward someone we say
you are just like me
your thoughts are my brothers
word matches word
how easy to be together.

When we are leaving someone we say
how strange you are
we cannot communicate
we can never agree
how hard, hard and weary to be together.

We are not different nor alike
but each strange in his leather body
sealed in skin and reaching out clumsy hands
and loving is an act
that cannot outlive
the open hand
the open eye
the door in the chest standing open.

Marge Piercy

Spider Webs

Spider webs are very delicate
And to remember.

A spider web is sometimes breaking.
It breaks when you take it
Or where it shakes in the wind
But always to remember
And delicate.

Delicate is when a thing is breaking
Sometimes when you take it
Or in the wind when it shakes.

Spider webs are to remember
 That things are delicate and sometimes break.
But after they break
 You remember.

Ray Fabrizio

Those Winter Sundays

Sundays too my father got up early
and put his clothes on in the blueblack cold,
then with cracked hands that ached
from labor in the weekday weather made
banked fires blaze. No one ever thanked him.

I'd wake and hear the cold splintering, breaking.
When the rooms were warm, he'd call,
and slowly I would rise and dress,
fearing the chronic angers of that house,

Speaking indifferently to him,
who had driven out the cold
and polished my good shoes as well.
What did I know, what did I know
of love's austere and lonely offices?

Robert Hayden

The Black Pebble

There went three children down to the shore,
    Down to the shore and back;
There was skipping Susan and bright-eyed Sam
    And little scowling Jack.

Susan found a white cockle-shell,
    The prettiest ever seen,
And Sam picked up a piece of glass
    Rounded and smooth and green.

But Jack found only a plain black pebble
    That lay by the rolling sea,
And that was all that ever he found;
    So back they went all three.

The cockle-shell they put on the table,
    The green glass on the shelf,
But the little black pebble that Jack had found,
    He kept it for himself.

James Reeves

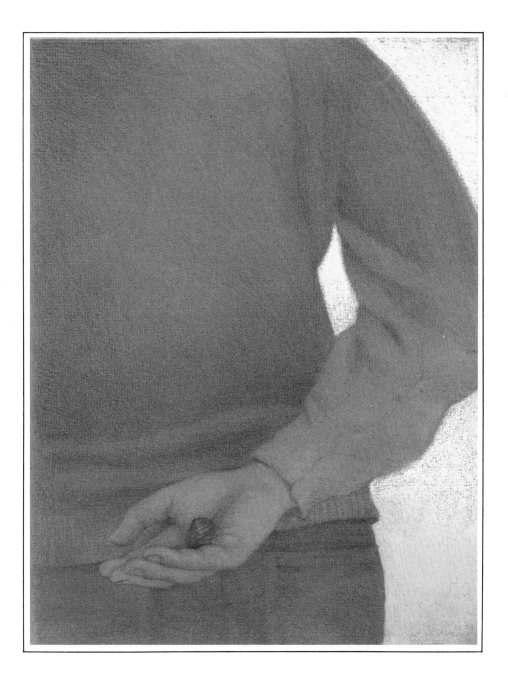

Forgive My Guilt

Not always sure what things called sins may be,
I am sure of one sin I have done.
It was years ago, and I was a boy,
I lay in the frostflowers with a gun,
The air ran blue as the flowers, I held my breath,
Two birds on golden legs slim as dream things
Ran like quicksilver on the golden sand,
My gun went off, they ran with broken wings
Into the sea, I ran to fetch them in,
But they swam with their heads high out to sea,
They cried like two sorrowful high flutes,
With jagged ivory bones where wings should be.

For days I heard them when I walked that headland
Crying out to their kind in the blue,
The other plovers were going over south
On silver wings leaving these broken two.
The cries went out one day; but I still hear them
Over all the sounds of sorrow in war or peace
I ever have heard, time cannot drown them,
Those slender flutes of sorrow never cease.
Two airy things forever denied the air!
I never knew how their lives at last were spilt,
But I have hoped for years all that is wild,
Airy, and beautiful will forgive my guilt.

Robert P. Tristram Coffin

My Papa's Waltz

The whisky on your breath
Could make a small boy dizzy;
But I hung on like death:
Such waltzing was not easy.

We romped until the pan
Slid from the kitchen shelf;
My mother's countenance
Could not unfrown itself.

The hand that held my wrist
Was battered on one knuckle;
At every step you missed
My right ear scraped a buckle.

You beat time on my head
With a palm caked hard by dirt,
Then waltzed me off to bed
Still clinging to your shirt.

Theodore Roethke

Loneliness

I was about to go, and said so;
And I had almost started for the door.
But he was all alone in the sugar-house,
And more lonely than he'd ever been before.
We'd talked for half an hour, almost,
About the price of sugar, and how I like my school,
And he had made me drink some syrup hot,
Telling me it was better that way than when cool.

And I agreed, and thanked him for it,
And said good-bye, and was about to go.
Want to see where I was born?
He asked me quickly. How to say no?

The sugar-house looked over miles of valley.
He pointed with a sticky finger to a patch of snow
Where he was born. The house, he said, was gone.
I can understand these people better, now I know.

Brooks Jenkins

Rough

My parents kept me from children who were rough
Who threw words like stones and who wore torn clothes.
Their thighs showed through rags. They ran in the street
And climbed cliffs and stripped by the country streams.

I feared more than tigers their muscles like iron
Their jerking hands and their knees tight on my arms.
I feared the salt coarse pointing of those boys
Who copied my lisp behind me on the road.

They were lithe, they sprang out behind hedges
Like dogs to bark at my world. They threw mud
While I looked the other way, pretending to smile.
I longed to forgive them, but they never smiled.

Stephen Spender

Boy at the Window

Seeing the snowman standing all alone
In dusk and cold is more than he can bear.
The small boy weeps to hear the wind prepare
A night of gnashings and enormous moan.
His tearful sight can hardly reach to where
The pale-faced figure with bitumen eyes
Returns him such a god-forsaken stare
As outcast Adam gave to Paradise.

The man of snow is, nonetheless, content,
Having no wish to go inside and die.
Still, he is moved to see the youngster cry.
Though frozen water is his element,
He melts enough to drop from one soft eye
A trickle of the purest rain, a tear
For the child at the bright pane surrounded by
Such warmth, such light, such love,
      and so much fear.

Richard Wilbur

Albert

Albert loved dogs mostly, though this was absurd
for they always slouched away when he touched their
     fur,
but once, perching on his shoulder, alighted a bird;

a bird alive as fire and magical as that day
when clear-eyed Heloise met Peter Abelard.
Though cats followed him, the bird never flew away.

And dogs pursued the cats which hunted the bird.
Albert loved dogs deeply but was jealously hurt
that they pursued him merely because of the bird;

the bird alive as fire and magical as that day.
So one morning he rises and murdered the bird
But then the cats vanished and the dogs went away.

Albert hated dogs after, though this was absurd.

Dannie Abse

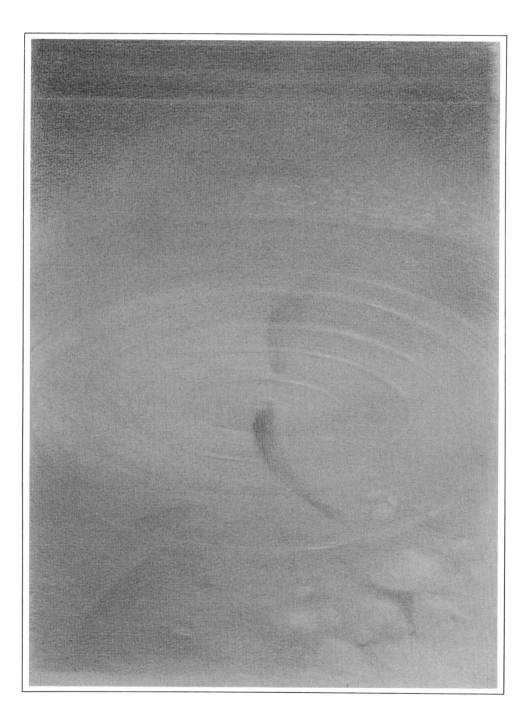

The Boy Fishing

I am cold and alone,
On my tree-root sitting as still as stone.
The fish come to my net. I scorned the sun,
The voices on the road, and they have gone.
My eyes are buried in the cold pond, under
The cold, spread leaves; my thoughts are silver-wet.
I have ten stickleback, a half-day's plunder,
Safe in my jar. I shall have ten more yet.

E. J. Scovell

Thumbprint

In the heel of my thumb
are whorls, whirls, wheels
in a unique design:
mine alone.
What a treasure to own!
My own flesh, my own feelings.
No other, however grand or base,
can ever contain the same.
My signature,
thumbing the pages of my time.
My universe key,
my singularity.
Impress, implant,
I am myself,
of all my atom parts I am the sum.
And out of my blood and my brain
I make my own interior weather,
my own sun and rain.
Imprint my mark upon the world,
whatever I shall become.

Eve Merriam

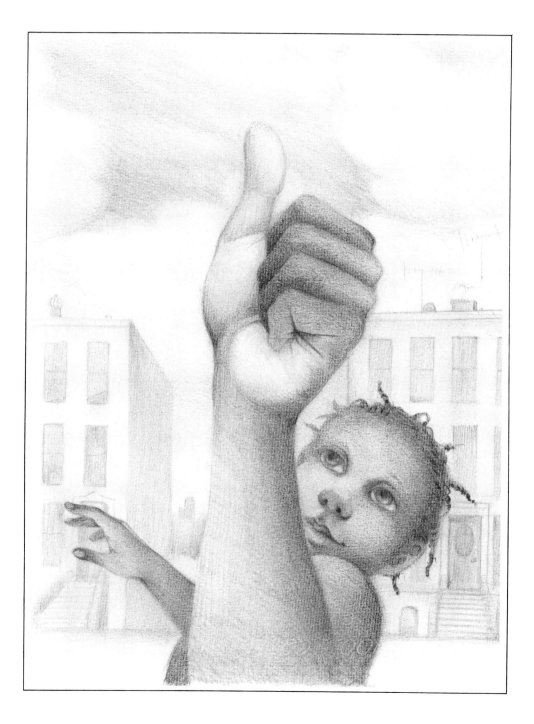

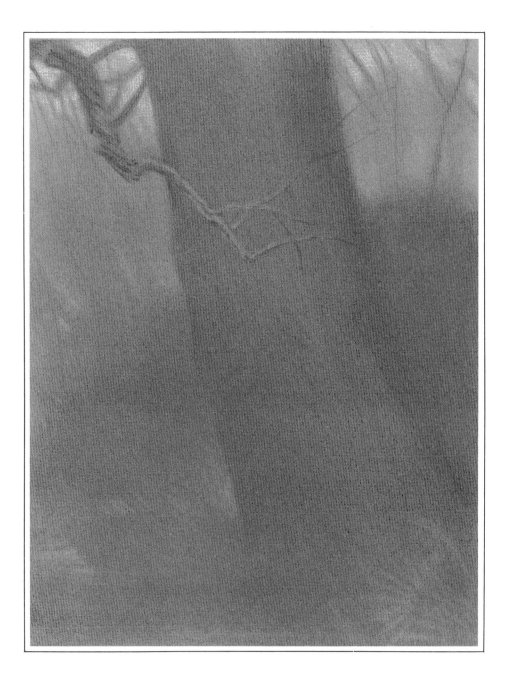

To Look at Any Thing

To look at any thing,
If you would know that thing,
You must look at it long:
To look at this green and say
'I have seen spring in these
Woods,' will not do—you must
Be the thing you see:
You must be the dark snakes of
Stems and ferny plumes of leaves,
You must enter in
To the small silences between
The leaves,
You must take your time
And touch the very peace
They issue from.

John Moffitt

Poem

I loved my friend.
He went away from me.
There's nothing more to say.
The poem ends,
Soft as it began—
I loved my friend:

Langston Hughes